IZZY BAIA

First published in 1998 by
Marino Books
an imprint of Mercier Press
16 Hume Street Dublin 2
Tel: (01) 661 5299; Fax: (01) 661 8583
E.mail: books@marino.ie

Trade enquiries to CMD Distribution
55A Spruce Avenue
Stillorgan Industrial Park
Blackrock County Dublin
Tel: (01) 294 2556; Fax: (01) 294 2564

ISBN 1 86023 075 X
10 9 8 7 6 5 4 3 2

A CIP record for this title is available
from the British Library

Cover design by Penhouse Design
Printed in Ireland by ColourBooks,
Baldoyle Industrial Estate, Dublin 13

Izzy Baia

AUTISM, LIFE
AND OTHER UNSOLVED MYSTERIES

Kevin Whelan

ACKNOWLEDGEMENTS

I would like to thank Margaret Murray and Ann Donohue of the Galway Association for Mentally Handicapped Children and also Pria Prendegast, formerly of the GAMHC. I don't know where I'd be today but for their intercession. Probably still on the dole.

Thanks to all at Marino for their help and expertise.

I also thank my brothers Michael, Eamonn and Sean, and my sister-in-law Marie, for reasons far too numerous – not to say unmentionable – here (or anywhere else).

I wish to acknowledge the kindness of friends and strangers. Thank you all.

ACKNOWLEDGMENTS

DEDICATION

For Anthony, Teresa, Brian, Eimear, Niall and Enda
O'Connor and Michael and Mary Whelan, parents. With
love.

And in memory of my uncle John Gallagher (1922–98),
bibliophile, of Fairfield, Crossmolina, County Mayo.

And of Ann Whelan, grandmother and scholar, Bally-
vaskin, County Clare.

'Include me out'
Sam Goldwyn (attrib.)

' AH ER EEE! Ah dee! Ehm er eh! '

Gibberish. Total gibberish.

He paces ahead of me down the Father Griffin Road. I close down on him as the early evening traffic streams home. The end of their working day is the beginning of mine. He's wearing his favourite outfit, a shiny green tracksuit.

He laughs, mutters some more of that gibberish, his voice a dull monotone, then glances suddenly at me.

'Slow down, Brian,' I say, catching up.

He flicks his fingers in front of his face, turning his head left, right, up, back.

We cross Wolfe Tone Bridge; he slows his pace on the narrow pavement.

It is the end of my first week as Brian's carer. What have I noticed? That he isn't much inclined to noticing me. He tends to stare off past my shoulder, as though gazing at an imaginary friend. He isn't being rude – he's being autistic. And all the other stuff – the nutty muttering to himself, the finger-flicking, the frenetic pacing – is just the way he is.

When the rest of us behave strangely, we can most often justify it: 'I was angry. I was pissed. I just broke up with my girlfriend. I just got back with my girlfriend. I hate my job. It's my sex drive.'

I'm not sure Brian has any idea of such normal excuses.

Turning into Quay Street he calms down somewhat. He claps his hands; his voice goes soft. He stands, waiting for me to catch up.

It's a Monday evening. Once again we walk down the Father Griffin Road. This time he lets me keep abreast of him, though I have a feeling that my presence has about as much reality to him as his shadow.

We pass Yeats College. Class is out for the day or they're taking a break. The college's students are here to be privately tutored through the Leaving Certificate curriculum – again – or to get a diploma of some kind.

The girls sit on the wall, waiting and smoking and talking. Some lounge on car bonnets. Brian breezes by, mumbling, clapping and jutting his head.

The lovely girls of Yeats College have not noticed him in his approach or in his passing. He barely registers. He might as well not exist. The irony, though, is that under normal circumstances he would make a lasting impression.

Brian is, by any standard (even that of Yeats College), very handsome. He hasn't the typical Irish colouring but is sallow-skinned. Also he is tall and slim with a swimmer's build. His hair is straight, medium-brown. He even has long eyelashes. In this he takes after his father, Anthony Kerry O'Connor.

We among the correctly functioning normal are innately quick and sharp – too much so, perhaps – in spotting differences in each other, differences we regard as useful, interesting and beautiful – or flawed, 'not right', wrong, improper. A subtle difference is sometimes all it takes – something about another's gait, perhaps. So we home in upon these quirks, decide that we will dislike or mistrust what we see and take it from there. From such attitudes comes much of the misery of this world.

I do it myself all the time. For instance, if I see someone with a tattoo I can't not think of neo-Nazis, thugs, sectarian killers or forget Truman Capote's observation when researching *In Cold Blood* that the one thing linking eighty-five per cent of the killers he interviewed in prison was that they each had one or more tattoos.

In other ways too I'll make a split-second judgement based on the tiniest of details.

I think that it might have something to do with my ancestors being, like yours, the hunter and the hunted. This wariness, I mean.

And because of this attitude, whole areas of human experience and contact are ignored, and real growth denied.

We are what we remember.
I began wary;
I held back, was frightened
by what my senses told me.
And, gradually, I learnt to be
watchful,
to be suspicious of them.

Brian is autistic.

There have always been autistic people. Autism (from the Greek word *autos* meaning 'self') was first described in 1943 by two doctors working independently of each other, Leo Kanner in Baltimore, USA and Hans Asperger in Vienna. Both described a condition characterised by the following: emotional remoteness, echolalia (the repeating of words and odd phrases) and exceptional observational abilities and memory recall.

Autistics are generally said to have what experts call 'mind blindness'; they don't and can't see the world as the rest of us do. Fearful of others, confounded by the world they find around them, autistics cope by adhering to a closely observed set of routines and apparently bizarre rituals, which, if upset, can cause them to react with a violent, screaming tantrum, what I called a 'mind-storm'. Among the things autistics particularly hate are loud noises. Think for a moment of just how noisy the average environment is. Now imagine what it must be like to be trapped – *trapped* – in a world where such things are a living nightmare.

Most, but not all, autistic people have some level of mental handicap. 'Asperger's Syndrome', however, describes a level of autism that does not stop the individual from having a normal education, finding employment, even raising a family.

What causes autism? Nobody really knows; it remains one of the great unsolved mysteries of twentieth-century medicine. Recent speculation (as of 1998) has centred on the side-effects of the three-in-one vaccine (measles, mumps, rubella) but even this has been discounted, at least by the British Medical Council. Another theory links chromosomes and multiple genes with autism, i.e. a genetic cause. Then again, another theory cites an excess of indoleacrylic acid, which is found in both yeast and milk and is believed to cause 'leaking' in the infant's gut, which in turn poisons the brain. What *is* known is that a gluten-free diet lessens the chances of a child developing some of the traits I've already listed as characterising autism.

Others have theorised that over-exposure to radiation in the womb causes autism. Or maternal rubella. Or encephalitis (inflammation of the coverings of the brain). Or trauma in the mother at birth. But again, this is so much guesswork.

Recent therapeutic research in America, however, suggests that by means of highly intensive one-on-one teaching – between child and parent or teacher – some autistic children can be taught to bond more closely with the parent and can thus outgrow some of the more 'obnoxious' aspects of the condition.

There are currently 800 registered autistic people in Ireland, a figure which increases by 25 per cent yearly and the majority are male. Europe's autistic population is estimated at one million – and rising.

In 1989 Dustin Hoffman won an Oscar as the autistic savant Raymond Babbitt in the movie *Rain Man*. Contrary to what is popularly believed, most autistics are not savant, i.e. do not have highly developed abilities in the visual arts or mathematics.

The following each has an autistic son: Sir Malcolm Arnold, British composer; Norman Stone, historian;

Kenzaburo Oë, Japan's Nobel Prize-winning writer; Les Murray, Australian poet; William Christopher ('Father Mulcahy' in *M*A*S*H*); Sylvester Stallone; and Nick Hornby, the English writer and author of *Fever Pitch* and *About a Boy*. Sir Malcolm's Fifth Symphony was inspired by the pain he felt at his son's condition; Les Murray has written poems about his son, Alexander, notably 'I Gotta Get Smart'.

WE'RE SITTING in Strawberry Fields. I'm sipping a coffee and wondering about things; Brian has a Coke and doughnut. I guess he's wondering about me – or not. Perhaps he simply accepts life as it happens, needing neither reasons nor explanations. There might be a lot to be said for such an attitude.

What I'm wondering about is this: will this latest occupation be as successful, or rather as unsuccessful, as some of the others I've found myself engaged in over the years. I tell myself that this time it had better be. I am twenty-nine years old.

Whether anyone knows it or not, I want very much to put all those apparently aimless (though occasionally highly educational) years behind me. The years of living in England, the nights in bedsits in Wood Green and Finsbury Park and Haringey in north London. Nights filled with the dread of being evicted by Irish landladies for missing one week's rent.

But this job is different. It has meaning.

I run through some of the jobs I had between January 1982 – when I was eighteen – and now, July 1993. 1982, the year I tried, truly, to be a good student general nurse, only to quit after one year because I knew then that I had no vocation, none at all, I was a con, a fraud. I had the stomach for the grisly aspects of life on the wards but my vocation was non-existent. The following years would see me flitting between Galway, Brentwood, Cambridge, London and Galway again. Always engaged in the sort of work no one seriously regarded as a suitable career for one Kevin Whelan: trainee assistant manager in a jewellers (Romford), from which I was fired after one week; swimming-pool cleaner; fast food flunkey in McDonald's (summer of '83, also Romford); Santa Claus (that's right); hotel night porter (Salthill, Galway); more fast food work (Salthill again); telephonist (Galway); parking-lot attendant (ditto); hospital cleaner (the heart-transplant unit of Papworth Hospital, Cambridge); bookshop assistant (Galway); delivering free property magazines on foot for the Prudential Building Society during the bitter winter of 1988, a terrible job, in the city of my birth (London); flyposter (still London).

And through all that time, I wrote, taking my typewriter with me to the ferry at Dun Laoghaire, to Holyhead, to catch the London train, arriving at cold stations in the dead of night – Victoria, Euston, Liverpool Street, whence to underground trains and buses and bedsits and Job Centres. These were my college years, and I learnt from them well.

And now, sitting opposite me is a sixteen-year-old autistic who knows nothing of shitty jobs or ambition or of feeling that, if you don't look like you're trying to make it, well then you're not making it at all.

'Cheers, Brian,' I say.

We clink cups.

AUTISTICS NEED routines and rituals the way Kennedy-assassination obsessives need the grassy knoll and a third gunman.

They just do.

For the last two weeks, I've let Brian keep to his routine. Like any other self-respecting autistic, once he has a routine established he feels safe, certain of its certainty.

But to my way of thinking, normal – non-autistic – routines are dull; they kill spontaneity. Routines make a prisoner of a man.

Something like autistic *glasnost* is called for: the liberation of comrade Brian O'Connor. Any life, autistic or not, should have some buzz, should have about it something of the quality of true living.

It is a Thursday evening during that annual orgy of excitement and despair called the Galway Races. The city is packed with punters, professional and amateur, wads of serious money held in elastic bands. Everyone listens to whispers and high-class whores check into the best hotels.

A very unroutine time in the life of the city.

In baseball terms, I'm about to throw Brian a curve ball. Forget the races; this is the Autistic World Series.

Here's my plan. Usually around now, six-thirty, we head up through Shop Street to get the Salthill bus from the stop outside the Irish Permanent in Eyre Square.

What I want Brian to do sounds simple. I want us to get the bus at the stop outside Hynes shoeshop, in Shop Street.

We've kept to the ESR (Eyre Square Routine) all week. Plus, we've – I've – obeyed all the others – the buying of Moro bars and cans of Cidona and bags of Monster Munch crisps in Raymond O'Brien's shop; heading down by Flood Street to get to Strawberry Fields for Cokes and chocolate doughnuts.

We move through the Shop Street throng. I'm wondering what, exactly, is the best way to handle this. It's not like my employer has provided me with a guidebook. The fact is, there isn't any guidebook.

Nearing Hynes and parallel with Eason's, I gently take him by the shoulder.

Be careful, I tell myself. Be very careful.

I must get the words I am about to say exactly right. What tone of voice shall I use? Cool, laid back. Yes.

'Listen, Brian,' – careful – 'we'll get the bus from here tonight.' I release his shoulder and put my hand on the bus-stop, as if it's the nicest, friendliest bus-stop in the world.

No big deal – for me, at least.

Not that Brian can know this. That which is perfectly normal and natural to me strikes the autistic as being insane, impractical, disordered. Wrong.

But my innocent words are out there now, logged inside his head. God only knows what sort of reading his mind is making of them.

He steps back, watching me carefully, like a man who has just had a handgun pulled on him and is considering his options. Careful, those beautiful eyes say, careful.

'Bus pass right here!' he shouts. And he whips it out, perfect in its new plastic coating, courtesy of the government and good for buses, trains, even state-subsidised ferries, entitling the holder and a companion to free travel. He holds it aloft, an autistic Neville Chamberlain home from visiting Adolf with the good news that no routines shall be violated. Routines in our time.

People hurry past. I smile indulgently at him.

'We'll wait for the bus here, Brian. It'll save us having to walk to the square.'

I might as well have fired a shot over his head. He stares, pivots; his eyes are wide and frightened as he stares up the street towards the safety of the square. There awaits salvation.

One half of him knows he must stay with me. But the other half, the rigid, unbending, bastard autistic brother whispers, 'Obey the routine. Therein lies safety. Obey, Brian!'

He steps towards me, takes my shoulder gently.

'Bus pass right here!' he repeats, his tone that of a psychiatric nurse coaxing a psychotic to put down the knife.

The Race Week mob hurries on.

Understanding comes to us all at some point, through those moments that define us by being startling, amusing, wrenching, glorious. Moments of love and heartbreak have this quality.

I'm not sure how often Brian has to deal with this kind of thing – hardly ever, I suspect. A shift might, just might, occur on this summer's evening as an illusion comes to an end and a life is changed for ever.

His face is pained as he begins to move away from me and out of this movie of my creation, *Nightmare On Shop Street*, written, produced and directed by K. W., starring as himself, co-starring Brian O'Connor, the director demanding that he act against type.

He paces back again.

'Kevin bus pass right here!' he announces in that ungrammatical way of his, hard and staccato. 'Let's go bus pass!'

'No, Brian,' I say, as conversationally as possible, 'We'll be getting the bus here,' and I stroke the bus-stop.

Off he goes again, only this time he looks as if he means it. Along the pavement he goes, stopping every other yard to gauge my reaction. I remain fixed at the stop.

'Bus, bus right here!' he shouts over the heads of the hurrying mob, who, being mostly Galwegian – that is, possessed of a certain easy cool and never fazed by episodes of weirdo behaviour or even moments of out-and-out insanity, especially during Race Week – ignore him. Though I notice that one or two commuters waiting nearby are watching us both closely, thinking, should we stick around? This could get interesting. But no, they move on.

I shake my head at Brian as he moves back to me to

renegotiate. His face is red as he jams a thumb into his mouth, as though to gnaw off some of his building anxiety, frustration, anger, autistic mania. Then he claps his hands, hard, gnaws some more on the thumb, paces.

People have started to cluster around the shop. If the bus is running on time, and it probably isn't given the traffic, we have at least another ten minutes to wait.

'Bus pass right here!' he says, as those gathered nearby stare from me to him.

His face contorts through expressions of pain, appeasement, incomprehension and finally disbelief, a face folding into mute sign language, as though there's a row of switches somewhere inside that unfathomable head of his and he's running madly back and forth, hoping to trigger the reaction that will convince me of my stupidity.

'Hmmmmm!' he says. Then, 'Bus pass right here!' his voice now lower than before. He paces back, bumps into pedestrians, oblivious of them.

An old woman stands nearby, smiling at me sympathetically, no doubt an expression I might have to get used to from the public. In fact, I'm probably going to have to get used to lots of things I wouldn't normally tolerate, if I want to hold on to this job. The thought of being on the dole again, or signing on, and the attendant feelings of worthlessness, guilt and shame – such thoughts send a shudder through me.

Am I being just a bit premature in trying to break him out of this particular routine? After all, what harm would it really do if we were to take the bus from Eyre Square? But no: there must be no going back now.

He has moved farther up the street. To whom should

I turn for help in a situation like this? Is there a patron saint of carers? Probably. For autistics? Should I ask the spirit of Kasper Hauser for guidance?

There is one man who might know what to do and that's good old Rocky Balboa himself – Sylvester 'Rambo' Stallone. After all, he has an autistic son Brian's age, named Seargoah.

(I can remember leaving the Odeon cinema in Romford, sometime in 1982, having just seen *Rocky III*, leaping on my Raleigh racer and burning through the streets of that Essex town, the wind in my hair, feeling that I could take on the whole world and win. I was eighteen, brave and sweaty with courage, because I knew then that I would soon quit nursing and do my own thing in life in my own way, though what that was I wasn't quite sure.)

And there's another thing – I did quit nursing, causing my parents I don't know how much worry, stress, sadness. Not that they ever said as much, of course. And, once my decision had been made, I remained in Romford for another year, doing some of the Mac jobs I mentioned earlier, refusing all offers of money to pay for my fare home.

And now here I am, a little over ten years later, wanting to do my damnedest to hold down this job, not just because I dread returning to the dole queue but because I want to redeem myself in my parents' eyes, in particular the eyes of my father – always kind, tolerant, doing his best to understand the dreams and ambitions that drove this particular son.

Rocky stayed in the ring; so will I.

Yet what can possibly disturb Brian so that he must stomp and roar in the middle of Shop Street?

I'd like to be sympathetic but now he's taking it too far. I really want to run at him and take him by the collar of that damned tracksuit and shake the frightened body inside it.

'All right, that's enough of this shit! Now cut it out!'

I mean, we'll do it your way – this time.

But no. That's exactly the kind of lazy, complacent attitude I want to rid myself of.

No: I'm in too deep now. So I stay put, while attempting to block out the strange looks the two of us are beginning to get. The ever-watchful normal world. What do they know?

And, more to the point, what do *I* know? What have I really taken on here? Am I, actually, insane? God knows I've had my doubts.

I stay standing by the bus-stop, letting my embarrassment – all this bullshit I have to deal with and a general feeling of being utterly pissed-off, Brian's rage, the mobbed street – letting it all wash in and over me.

Those nearest me must be thinking that I'm Brian's brother. Or something. I smile at that, not entirely sure why.

Meanwhile, little brother paces backwards and forwards.

And then it happens, like a miracle. From the end of the street I hear the low, familiar rumble of the Salthill bus. It eases by Dillon's Jewellers at the top of William Street as it makes its slow progress towards us.

Brian, in his hyper-alert autistic way has spotted it at the same time.

'Bus pass!' A smile of huge relief settles over his face. He strides towards me, the pass held high. A winner. We both are.

I board the bus with a fleeting sense of triumph, fleeting because I know that the same scene will probably be repeated the next evening. But that's tomorrow. Today I put a crack in the routine.

The noise and clamour of a summer street
as it pulses with life. The air hums with
a pulsing electrical stink; everything is too fast.
Rituals should be sacred.
In Autistland, everything follows as it
   should.

I HAVE NOTICED that when we visit Eason's bookshop, Brian is drawn to the First Aid shelf.

I watch as, in his slender hands, he takes down the *Red Cross First Aid Book* and cradles it. It is always lovely to see anyone handle a book with respect. A dusty old bibliophile couldn't be more reverential. His expression is sombre, even intellectual. Watching him like this, it would be easy to mistake Brian for one of the university's earnest young medical students.

But Brian is never going to be a medical student. And that *never* is as permanent as stone.

He scrutinises a scene representing a car crash.

'Man hurt leg,' he tells me, his face grave. Then he does a fantastic thing – for an autistic, I mean: he looks clear into my eyes, holds my gaze (as though to check that I'm paying close attention), then moves on to the next page.

This time we see an old woman lying slumped against a wall, a victim of shock or stroke. It isn't as literal as the other pictures – there is no blood or gaping wounds – and this bothers him.

'Happened?' he asks. Then, 'lady sick.'

And I'm standing there thinking, what if . . . ?

I put my arm around his shoulder. 'Let's go and get

our drinks, shall we?'

'Yeah,' he says, and he replaces the book carefully back upon the shelf.

All that an individual might have
 been,
have given,
been part of.
All that contained for ever.
Tender ritual holding me;
tenderly enfolding me.

AUTISTICS ARE the aristocrats of the mentally handicapped (though not all autistics have a mental handicap).

Look closely at the autistic manner. Their bearing is aloof, remote, guarded – fascinating. They are an élite ruled by rituals meaningless to the onlooker. It is like a secret etiquette of the mind.

Imperious and sometimes grave, caring not whether they are deemed to 'fit in', or whether they meet with your approval, they live wholly within themselves and for themselves. They are beyond us; they are beyond our rules; they are beyond our way of being.

Who really wants to know another
  completely?
The real self is probably more bearable
  hidden than exposed,
Yet . . . as lonely and rare as an orchid on Mars.

I THINK THAT autistics are not unlike black holes, those once fabulous stars in deep space that somehow collapsed in upon themselves, dragging matter into their dense, unfathomable cores; holding within their special light, for ever.

Into Brian's head go the pictures in the *Red Cross First Aid Book* and car names, every name you could possibly think of, but specifically Opel, Peugeot, Nissan, Toyota, Ford. On a winter's night I test Brian, pointing to a dark blur moving over O'Brien's Bridge, one hundred yards distant.

'Brian, what sort of car is that?'

'Opel Corsa,' comes his answer as my question ends.

The normal world scurries about its business, the streets filled with their jabbering. What are any of them saying, really? About whom are they speaking?

I'M WALKING into town along the Father Griffin Road without Brian this time – it's Saturday – when two fourteen-year-old girls pass me by on their bikes. One of them veers into the centre of the road, forcing the driver in the car following to make two gentle toots on the horn to draw their attention – beep! beep! – as he tries to pass.

The second he finishes, the girl on the outside, the one in the middle of the road, turns her head in his direction and screams in the kind of hard Galway accent that can cut through sheet metal, 'Ah, fuck off!'

The driver overtakes, but gingerly, as the other girl, the one nearest me, turns and starts screaming at him too.

'Ah, fuck up!' Her face is a red fury.

And together they speed away, as though in pursuit.

WE SIT OPPOSITE each other in Lynch's café. Brian separates a packet of Fruit Gums and arranges them, by colour, in meticulous matching vertical lines, his attention as thorough as a Buddhist monk conducting the Zen tea ceremony.

I sip my coffee, enjoying the irony of the situation. The fact is, I love conversation, I sometimes talk too much, yet here I am being taught a lesson in patience, learning how to sit alongside another who demands nothing from me in the way of chat, conversation, talk – call it what you like. One, indeed, who demands nothing from me but to be me.

I leaf through Colin Wilson's *Unsolved Mysteries – Past and Present*. Only the week before I had come across one of those bargain books, *The Amazing Book Of Mazes*. As a joke, to make a visual pun, I put Francesca Happé's academic work *Autism* between *Unsolved Mysteries* and *Mazes*. Because once you start thinking about autism you realise that one of the reasons why so little is know about the condition's origins is that it's a modern riddle, a puzzle; it is an intellectual maze with countless false turns and dead ends.

The three books take their place in a section of my library lined with literature on the strange, the bizarre, the baffling. *Curiosa*.

TONIGHT A WOMAN who has seen me in Brian's company, asked, 'Is he your brother?' I was, of course, flattered, but said, 'No, Brian isn't my brother. I'm his carer. I look after him for a couple of hours each evening.'

'He's your friend?' she persisted.

To which the only honest answer I could have given was, 'Well, I like him a lot.'

But a friend?

The only friends I was ever really close to are distant memories from my childhood in Oxfordshire. There were Jeremy Westerby, Christopher Wellington and Andrew Young, from prep school, and later John Adams, from my time in Burford Grammar School. I lost contact with all of them once my family moved to Ireland. In Galway I found it harder than ever to make new friends. And being regarded as English hardly helped.

I had to make up my own friends, and found them in books. I withdrew into Enid Blyton and Alfred Hitchcock, James Herbert and, for some reason, prison memoirs, *Papillon*, *Midnight Express*, *Borstal Boy*. My stockpile of books became my weapons against a world that taunted anyone considered even slightly different. The covers of each volume were like secret doors into wonderful and exciting worlds, where no one took the piss ('only slagging') or obeyed the tyranny of the peer group.

My teenage years: a perfect background for the job I now had. What was autism but the mind's involuntary protest, a mental revolt, against the cruelty, meanness and cowardice of such a world?

The boarders at my secondary school were a category unto themselves. Farmers' sons, they couldn't decide if they hated me or admired me. While they wore the sensible jumper and slacks their mammies had bought in Dunnes Stores, I wore black clothes and Mod ties. I listened to ska music and Gary Numan when they were considered mutually exclusive. I can still hear those country voices chiding me, trying to get a reaction to bad-mouthing Numan.

They all seemed to be obsessed in one way or another with homosexuality and no doubt they had their worries about me, though I surely puzzled them, being neither nerdy – I wasn't short or fat; I didn't wear glasses and I wasn't a swot – but markedly different, buzzing out of the school gates on my beat-up Honda 50, cruising down Taylor's Hill, longing to stop and chat with one of the 'Taylor's girls' from the Dominican convent but somehow always kept just outside their circle of secret talk.

And now here was Brian, almost an extreme form of myself in those days. But I had learnt well from them and, by one of those circuitous routes that life often takes you down, it had brought me into his life as his carer, his minder, his 'friend'.

My friend never said anything, unless it was to ask for something he wanted, his vocabulary limited – with me – to 'Moro, Fruit Gums, bus pass,' or variations on the same.

It didn't mean though that I didn't want to know Brian as a friend, to be able to tell him things, to share words on hopes and dreams, to just sit and bullshit with each other or to say something, however brief, about how beautiful it was to experience life fully, to be part of the world, whatever its faults.

Like? Like the delicious feeling of anticipation before a date: those moments before her arrival, knowing that she will push through the bar's doors just for you.

Like? Like the silly, even banal things you will talk about, the strange experiences before this other came into your life.

Like? Like glancing at your watch while she goes to the toilet and seeing that only twenty minutes have passed and that you both have more time for drinking, for remembering, for laughter and wonder, for more of that togetherness, that beginning of friendship.

I don't understand
these ways of being
that matter to them;
above all else, all else that
is logical and makes sense,
I mean.

HERE IS THE paradox of Brian O'Connor and his kind:

the autistic purity, to be born pure and remain pure,
uncontaminated by normal vices – or virtues
as a butterfly tapping against a summer screen is pure,
as a snowflake melting silently is pure, as Guinness is
pure
living devoid of schemes, ambitions, self-aggrandising
motives
weirdly innocent
and annoying, occasionally violent, utterly perplexing

Brian and those eight hundred other Irish autistics and
their brothers and sisters in mind – American, English,
Welsh, Spanish, German, Danish, Kenyan, Indian, Mexican,
Israeli, Arab, Japanese, Australian. All of that, regardless
of race, colour, religious vocation, all jabbering and
staring and finger-flicking, and baffling in their uniquely
autistic way.

    Being themselves. Being as we were meant to be.

    The way we could be, only we – you reading this and
me writing it – are retarded. We're not the handicapped,
are we?

Taking others at face value, without inhibition.

Weird.

No concerns with normal concerns. ('I don't like them/ him/her/that because . . . ')

Meanwhile, I walk alongside him into town but no one thinks to stare at me because I've mastered the same behaviour they've mastered. I'm not the one waving his hands in front of his face and talking gibberish.

People, though, can be kinder that expected. Brian might get stared at now and then but never with anything like cruelty. And I've yet to hear anyone make a cutting remark to him. Look: what you see with an autistic is exactly what you get. They can't be found out because they're not hiding anything.

Meanwhile, I keep my head down, metaphorically speaking. I let others see only what I want them to see. Don't you?

He's finally said something.

He's inside his house having a mindstorm. When that happens nothing can be done to placate him. His father Anthony keeps after him through the house as his eldest son flails his arms, strikes out at his brothers, roars, fumes, his face red and sweaty. He stomps down into the kitchen, pummels his mother, roars some more. We all do our best to reason with him but the idea of reasoning with an autistic in full mindstorm-mode is utterly pointless, like Lear roaring at the storm. I know that there isn't a whole lot I can do. If he doesn't listen to his father, he's unlikely to pay any attention to me. Still, I've never seen Brian this bad before.

I step outside. It's one of those near perfect summer evenings, not too hot, not too cool. I sit on the wall, watching the local children playing. But being outside doesn't stop the action coming from inside being heard. He shouts at Anthony, screams some more. He's upstairs now, and I imagine his face as he smashes his fists into the thin walls, his expression contorted in a thrashing fury.

I take a deep breath and am letting it out when I hear a loud, splintering sound – the bathroom mirror.

I get off the wall, consider the logic of going back inside to help out. I get as far as the door, push it open.

He's downstairs now, flicking his fingers. His face has returned to its normal colour. He fetches his coat, kisses his mother on the cheek and catches up with me as I walk out the drive.

He is sniffling, apparently ashamed.

'Brian be good very sorry!' he tells me as we make it on to the main road.

'Tell it to your parents, especially your dad,' I say.

'Brian be good very sorry.'

Born without the necessary façades of others.
No front here, no act, no obvious disguise.
As human as anyone else,
as pissed-off and fucked up
as anyone else.
Not that I'm asking for any kind of
special pleading.
In Austisland, we exist in time outside the
normal world. There, it is not necessary to
lie or to disguise my true self,
nor deny who I am, even if, like you,
I'm not entirely
sure of the who or the am.

ANOTHER EVENING.

We're passing down Shop Street when he stops before a video monitor in the window of Zhivago Records.

'*Jurassic Park!*' he says.

'You're wrong, Brian,' I say because I'm the film buff around here.

'*Jurassic Park*,' he repeats, watching the video closely.

To indulge him, I pretend that he's right and decide to take a closer look. All I can see is some sort of high-tech lab, soft lighting on smooth steel surfaces. Two men sit at some sort of control panel, like a space-age meeting between Beckett's *Godot* and Pinter's *Caretaker*. It isn't *Jurassic Park* because I know for a fact he's only seen the movie once, and that was when I took Brian and his brothers Enda and Niall to see it in the Claddagh Palace in Nile Lodge.

Then the scene changes. We're still in the lab only now there's a fat guy sneaking around, a very furtive fat guy sneaking around. Now he's removing some top-secret-looking stuff from the inside of some sort of container.

It's the scene in *Jurassic Park* when Nedry steals the dinosaur embryos!

'You're exactly right, Brian,' I say, patting him on the back.

'*Jurassic Park*,' he repeats, slowly, as though speaking to a child.

If the normal can't comprehend something,
then the normal way is not to comprehend it.
They call this 'saving face'.

BACK WHEN I was a flyposter (in London) I lived in a bedsit in Haringey. My days were spent 'ducking and diving' (as Londoners say) from the attentions of the Metropolitan Police. I was Bill Posters himself, working the West End – Soho, Covent Garden, Cambridge Circus, the King's Road, Knightsbridge and most of north London, particularly Finsbury Park and the Holloway Road. The gig paid in cash, no tax, and kept my Meath landlady off my back.

It was a Saturday and I was returning from Kensington, travelling the Piccadilly Line on the underground, when the train suddenly took aboard fifty or so football supporters. They were all white, in their twenties and thirties, and they took up all the space in the narrow carriage, joshing and leaning into each other. Then, on cue, they started to roar – no other word for it – the following:

'We are animals! We are animals!'

I glanced (and it was only that: an innocent appraisal) at the fellow – the 'animal' – in the seat next to me. He looked like an estate agent, a bank clerk or a radiologist on his day off, in his crisp polo shirt and pressed Levis.

'*We are animals! We are animals!*' he and the others continued as the train sped under the capital.

'UNDERSTANDING is the beginning of everything,' wrote the American poet, story-writer and novelist, Charles Bukowski. I think that if I could begin to understand those apparently beyond my understanding – and they might as well be autistic as not – I had better begin now. It is never too late to have your own way of seeing the world radically challenged.

Some questions:

What goes on inside autistic people's heads?

What do they dream about?

What is a dream to an autistic? And do they wonder about them afterwards?

Do they wonder?

Think of a Rubik's cube which is by turns a jigsaw and now a puzzle no one can solve because no one has yet to think of a solution – because they're not sure it is a puzzle.

My maze analogy.

Unsolved Mysteries – Past and Present.

Colin Wilson's first book, published when he was just twenty-four, was called *The Outsider*. It was a critically acclaimed study of the alienated outsider in modern literature.

WHEN I WAS a child – I would have been nine or ten – I thought in rather an unusual way. I think this might in part have had something to do with a distinctly eccentric childhood. Even the names of the people I knew were somehow strange. There were Stews and Parrotts and Eagers and Sharplys (both doctors), and Bigg and Flower (dentists). Then there was the time I was admitted to the Nuffield Orthopaedic Hospital in Oxford because something had turned up in an X-ray of my left knee. The surgeons removed a length of paperclip. How it got there none of us knew but apparently it had been lodged deep inside the joint for two years, causing me terrible pain from time to time.

I shared the ward with a haemophiliac called Ainsley French. 'If I get even a little cut I'll bleed to death,' and he'd smile.

While all this was happening, I started wondering about the planet I was living on. We had a huge plum tree in the back of our garden in Carterton and I would sit under it and wonder what the world would be like if it didn't exist. Not just that; what if the solar system and all the galaxies didn't exist? I even tried to imagine what sort of colour it would be. I decided that it couldn't be black because space was black and, in my thinking, if the galaxies didn't exist then it followed that neither could space.

Finally, I pictured a sterile white expanse of nothing-ness. White was as close as I could get to an invisible colour. My childish mind thought in conundrums. But I still needed some answers.

And so it was with the autistic mind. No answers. No clues. No nothing.

Why does he persist with these questions?
He probes too much.
Why can't he be?
Why can't he leave it all alone?

NEVER TO SPEAK of dreams, ambitions, even banal aspi-
rations; never to sing the plain notes of living and
growing. No biases aired, no doubts revealed, no enthusi-
asms voiced. No 'wouldn't it be great if . . . '

Nearly every waking moment tuned to autistic anxiety,
to sudden giddy delight.

Or rage.

Think about what I call a mindstorm, as waves of
frustration, anger, fear and terror sweep through the
autistic's being, so that in seconds he is a thrashing,
roaring, body of rage. (And if you don't think an autistic
is capable of serious physical violence, of causing real
pain and injury, then you risk seeing them as idealised
beings but not as individuals.)

I've seen Brian in just such moments since the mirror-
breaking incident, his face and body contorted as though
in some vain attempt at clearing it from his system.

And as suddenly as it occurs . . . a clearing, a sooth-
ing; a return to calm.

'Sorry be good!'

His face flushed as he leaves the house, following me.
Exactly what am I to him, anyway?

'Kevin.'

Once I asked him: 'Brian, what's my surname? If your name is O'Connor, what's my name?'

'Kevin.'

'Kevin Whelan.'

'Yeah.'

'So what's my name again?'

'Kevin.'

'Kevin what?'

'Kevin what, yeah.'

'Never mind, Brian.'

And there is our paradox, one of many, of course. That I know nearly all there is to know about him and he knows only two things about me. My first name. And that I call to his house at five-fifteen every weekday evening to take him into town.

And to Brian, I guess that's all he needs to know.

A world tuned to its
own electrical buzz.
Not so in Austistland.
There everything is calm;
there, everything is just as it should be.
Here, though, among the normal,
the very air is charged.

To AVOID TRAFFIC, I cycle through the one-way system beside Cathedral Buildings. The road takes a sharp right turn that leads to Nuns' Island (which is not an island but the site of a convent housing an enclosed order of nuns). I arrive at the O'Connors in about eight minutes.

Ahead of me two trucks with long trailers are parked facing each other. One truck is half-on, half-off the pavement; the other faces towards town, taking up most of the narrow road. The first truck is leaving a depot. It's a Robin Hood and Little John on the bridge face-off.

So much for my short cut. I dismount and push the bike between them. I can see the drivers. They've left their cabs and are gesticulating wildly at each other. They're each in their forties, overweight, and with matching heads of thick, greasy dark hair. They could be brothers.

'Look here,' one of them is saying, 'I have the right of way.' From this I take it that he's the one in the lorry going towards the city, the one with most of his truck in the road. 'This is a one-way system, in case you haven't noticed,' he adds.

'Sure amn't I only tryin' to back out of the depot and go about me business?' says the other driver.

'So back up and let me pass so,' says the first one. He has a point.

'Why can't you back up?'

'Cause I got here first and it's a one-way system.'

'Where are you from, anyhow?'

'I'm a Roscommon man!'

'And I'm a Meath man!'

Their faces are red as I pass between them. I get back on the bike, thinking of the car stickers saying 'I'm for peace.' In the North, that is.

'And I'm a Roscommon man!' is the last thing I hear as I pedal away.

A STORM IS approaching. I don't mean of the autistic kind but the real thing: rain, sleet, hail, possibly even snow sent down in hard winds and lightning bolts.

We take a booth in Eddie Rockets at the corner of Eglinton Street.

Brian glances out of the window while the waiter takes our order. He has a hypersensitivity to barometric pressure. And if there's one thing that really scares him, it's a storm.

We both hear it at the same time: a low rumble, far off, followed by a scatter of raindrops. Brian's face creases in anxiety. To his way of thinking a storm is a personal physical attack on him. The windows are large and wide; it's as if we're watching from inside a huge TV. Then, as though a black cloth had been draped over the fading sun, another rumble is heard.

People are leaving their offices – though they ought to have enough sense to stay exactly where they are – and scurrying in all directions. Outside, other pedestrians quicken their pace, like extras in a movie playing at the wrong speed.

Our drinks arrive but Brian ignores them. Even his Fruit Gums wait unwrapped. It's then that I notice it: the slightest of tremors in his hands, as though he has picked up the storm's electrical current in the tips of his fingers.

People now rush in from outside, laughing nervously as a massive boom rocks through the street. 'That was close! We got here just in time.' Eddie Cochran is playing over the PA 'Summertime Blues'. The diner becomes quiet. We are all expectant.

Brian glances fretfully at the ever darkening street. Then, as though on cue, raindrops splatter hard on the windows, slide down, returning as hail.

'Boom.'

'*Boom!*'

I picture the storm rolling in from the Corrib, from its obscure lakes, from the Atlantic, and just then the whole junction is lit with lightning. It seems to split the sky and the rain and sleet fall hard.

The tremor in Brian's hands is worse now. I notice him watching a couple huddled together at the corner of Francis Street as others splash down the pavement, the lightning cracking and ripping in their wake.

'*Happened!*' Brian cries as suddenly all the lights inside the diner go off, the jukebox shuts down and for all of three seconds we're in darkness.

'*Bing!*'

And like that the light and the music return as Eddie Cochran sings 'I'd like to help yer son but yer too young to vote.'

Brian looks frantically at me, as if I have the power to stop the storm.

All I can do is sympathise. I reach across the table and take his hands, hold them. 'You're safe here, Brian.

Nothing is going to hurt you.'

But I can read his eyes and they are saying, 'It's useless; a nightmare has come to life.'

The storm continues, all crack and rip of a huge snare drum. The gutters are awash as it rolls and booms, shaking the city.

And then, as suddenly as it arrived, the storm has blown itself out. No storm, of whatever kind, lasts any longer than it has to.

'Wind over?' he asks.

'Wind over,' and I grip his hands.

'Wind over,' he repeats as he turns his head to look upon the junction.

The night electric, while vertical sheets
of rain bind the junction like wire cages
made from water, holding terror.

WE LEAVE THE house and continue down Whitestrand Avenue to wait for the bus at Nile Lodge. For the last few days I've noticed a playful look on his face as he peers ahead. Only, now that I think about it, I realise that I have seen this particular expression before, not just on Brian but on other children with a mental handicap. The only word I can think of to describe it is 'worshipful'.

'Is ee bi ya!' he says. More gibberish.

But about those other children ... I once worked in the deaf unit of a special school. All six of the children communicated using a small vocabulary of signs. (There is a specialised sign language for deaf or hearing-impaired children with a mental handicap.)

And the children liked to communicate. Just because they were handicapped didn't mean that they didn't have something to say.

There was one little girl in particular. She was, interestingly enough, autistic (autism is a condition that occurs four times out of five in boys).

I'll call her Jean. She was a strikingly beautiful child, with blonde hair framing a face as soft and delicate as a porcelain figurine. (And here's another thing. Generation after generation of researchers have commented on the often exceptional beauty of autistic children.)

One of the things Jean most enjoyed doing was sitting cross-legged in the playroom. There she would reach with her hands into empty space, a wistful smile playing on her lips. It was as though she were engaged in a solitary game of blindman's bluff; there was about her manner an eager grasping for something apparently within her reach but invisible.

Although Jean was prone, like all autistic children, to her own mindstorms, on these occasions she always looked nothing less than ecstatic. Peacefully she sat, her frustrations apparently non-existent.

Gingerly then her delicate fingers would probe the air and then she would start to giggle. It was as though the air itself was her playmate. When she had composed herself, she would set about with her probing once more, all the time her concentration total, centred on . . .

On what?

And the other children in the unit, at different times and in almost identical ways, made the same motions with their hands and their eyes held the same ecstatic look.

It was only a year later, while thumbing through John Cornwell's *Powers of Darkness, Powers of Light*, with lengthy chapters on the phenomenon of Marian visions at Medjugorje that I saw, in the pictures accompanying the text, the same beatific, ecstatic expressions on the faces of the young visionaries, as they gazed in supplication at what they believed was the Virgin Mary.

I used, then, to wonder about Jean and the other children. Was it really possible that they too were seeing something truly fantastic? Something so out of this world, so beautiful that we – the normal – had been denied seeing or had lost the ability to see?

I even considered the possibility of angels . . . and promptly chided myself.

Angels! Angels, indeed.

Brian and I reached the bus-stop at Nile Lodge. He was still at it, his head now tilted to one side, smiling all the while.

'Iss ee bi ya.'

(I'm almost reminded of Robert De Niro as the lonely and demented Travis Bickle in the Paul Schrader-scripted Martin Scorsese film *Taxi Driver*. Travis standing alone in his room, asking his mirror, 'You talkin' to me? Well I'm the only one here.')

Now, being a practical kind of man (that is, when it suits me), I think that I just might have a perfectly logical explanation for this – what should I call it? – beatific mumbling carry-on.

According to Brian's mother, Teresa, he enjoys hearing foreign languages on TV. Brian has even been known to repeat unfamiliar foreign words with all the meaning he would give to English (which can be a lot of or, yes, total gibberish). I've heard him do it myself. It sounds like nothing less than a kind of nutty autistic Esperanto.

'Iss eeeee bii ya!' Brian says, apparently to the bus-stop.

'Brian, who are you talking to?'

'Iss eee bi ya.'

I guess this is what the Chinese sage Lao Tzu meant when he remarked in the *Tao Te Ching*, 'Names can name no lasting name.'

'Thanks for clearing that up,' I say as the bus arrives.

Who?

Me, of course.

Trust him to ask.

WE'RE SITTING in a city-centre restaurant finishing our drinks and, as happens every evening, Brian says, 'Toilet?' It's one routine and ritual I'm not interesting in breaking him out of.

This time, I hold my hand up. I want him to wait a while. Because just moments before a middle-aged man had passed our table, had looked at us, I felt, too closely, and continued to the stairs in the direction of the men's toilets.

Brian pops another Fruit Gum into his mouth and sits chewing with his hands resting patiently in his lap.

At least five minutes pass.

'Wait here a moment, Brian. There's something I have to check on.'

I leave the table and move swiftly but quietly up the stairs. When I reach the toilets, I open the door carefully and peer inside. The solitary stall door is marked 'engaged'.

I ease the door closed and return to Brian.

'There's a man in the toilet, Brian. We'll wait a while until he leaves. '

'Man goes.'

Five minutes later, I repeat the exercise. I'd rather be paranoid than know it's true. Once again 'engaged'.

'Go toilet?' he asks.

I glance up the stairs. Everyone deserves the benefit of the doubt. But no one appears.

'Listen, Brian, you can go to the toilets in the Cellar,' I say, referring to a nearby bar.

'Toilet?' He looks at me hard. He deserves some sort of explanation.

'Not here, Brian. I think that man we saw going up the stairs ten minutes ago is a bad man.'

'Man bad.' He makes it a statement.

'That's right. Let's get out of here.'

Facing the world in total openness.
Living and seeing without guile.
Vulnerable.

I'm SITTING at the counter in a local bar, a place I seldom visit, but here I am. I order a Guinness as two building labourers from a nearby site take seats at the other end of the counter. In the top righthand corner is a TV. The RTE *Nine O'Clock News* is about to start when the barmaid takes the remote control and flicks to Channel 4. I hope that this means she, like me, wants to watch this week's episode of *ER*.

She brings me my pint; then, as though she can read my mind, says to the other two, whom she apparently know as regulars, 'I'm going to watch *ER*.' I smile to myself at the way she tells them. Women who work in bars are among the few occupations I really respect and admire (the others are nurses, waitresses, shop assistants and taxi drivers). At any moment barmaids may be called upon to settle fights, rights and arguments; be surrogate mothers, sisters, wives, girl friends; psychoanalysts, therapists and new best friend. All while trying to maintain a professional emotional distance from the drinker.

One of the labourers settles his pint on the bar, his face a mask of disgust.

'So yer gonna watch *ER* so?' he asks, shifting his big

butt on the stool.

'That's right,' says the barmaid.

'What about the news and *Prime Time?*' says the other fellow, whom I wouldn't have pegged as a current affairs type. Though, as I had often discovered, appearances are deceptive.

'Sure won't that only be more stuff about the North and the ceasefire and all the rest of it? I'm sick of listening to them all.'

'So you're going to watch that *ER* so?' says the first labourer.

'That's right.'

The two of them looked set to spit.

'Sure won't that thing be only full of them blacks and Indians and queers,' says the second fellow, looking at his friend for back-up.

'Well I like *ER*,' she tells them and, as though to end the conversation, she leaves the remote control on a shelf over the cash register and walks down to my end of the counter.

'I want to watch *ER* too,' I whisper to her.

The show's opening scene comes on.

The two critics shake heads in disgust and return to their drinking.

I looked at them. Just regular guys. Gas men. Not bad, really. I believed that.

Sipping my pint, I realised that that was just the trouble. It was one of the reasons why I never minded drinking alone: it meant not having to listen to other people's bullshit. Regular guys. I'd been in enough bars over the years to recognise the type, all regular hate and regular insanity, all holding fast to their own truths. But what most people seemed to accept as the truth was whatever sat most comfortably with their own biases and, in particular, prejudices, and once a version of this truth was made, then they lived their lives by it, regardless of any contradictory evidence.

The labourers, the barmaid and myself were all players in a world Brian knew nothing of, and did not understand as others like him could not understand.

No escape from these,
the 'normal'.
I would rather withdraw
farther into my solitary core,
exult in ritual, however banal.
I wish only for separation from them
and their way of being.
And yet to consider, even for a moment,
such notions, was to be singled out by
them, to be labelled on their terms.
I've heard it all before:
'Retarded'
'Abnormal'
'Weirdo'
'Idiot'
'Nut'
'Freak'
Autistic.

You never can tell when a mindstorm will hit.

Inside the O'Connors' kitchen on this September evening he stomps. It's a bad one; his face is terribly flushed; sweat beads on his forehead.

Anthony steps between mother and son; he has her in a headlock. I get between them, pulling at Brian, doing my best to loosen his grip.

'Brian, you're hurting me!' Teresa says.

I separate them just as toast pops up from the toaster. It may be five-thirty but in autist-time that doesn't mean a thing; he missed his breakfast this morning so logically, whether he's hungry or not, he has to eat his breakfast now. I don't even want to ask how he missed it before, not because his mother hadn't made him one, that's for sure.

'Throw toast on the floor!' he screams and down the toast goes. I guess he isn't too bothered about breakfast then.

'Brian, for God's sake!' I feel useless saying it but feel I have to make some sort of comment.

I stand next to Anthony. We're both trying to anticipate his next move. Suddenly Brian has a breakfast side plate in his hands and throws it, full force, at the door, missing his mother by inches.

'Go shopping Dunnes Stores!' he cries.

So that's it: he's got it into his head that they should be going shopping. Routine and ritual again.

'No,' his mother tells him, with incredible patience. 'Go shopping Saturday,' Teresa says, lapsing into the useful staccato we all use with him, wittingly recreating his own speech patterns.

Outside, the neighbourhood children gather with Brian's brothers. They know something's up.

I close the front door. The action has moved into the narrow front hall. Suddenly, he has his mother by the wrists again, pinning her to the wall.

'Please, Brian!' she says.

The smell of his sweat is thick in the air. His shirt is soaked through.

'Go shopping Dunnes Stores?'

'No, Brian,' Teresa answers.

'That's it! I'm going to call the guards,' Anthony says and he really looks as if he means it too.

'Call the guards go shopping Dunnes Stores?'

He peers desperately into his mother's eyes. Finally, we manage to pull him away. Anthony and I let him go and the three of us stand facing each other. Then, wap! Brian slaps Anthony in the face.

'*That's it!*' Anthony says. Now he really looks like he's going to make that call. He goes to the phone, Brian watching him, his face slick with wet. His father dials not for the guards but instead for a service provided by the mentally handicapped association that looks after Brian's education and provide weekend respite. The service is a new thing, designed for just such emergencies. Anthony's hoping they'll send someone around to take Brian into one of their group homes for the night. He has the rest of his family to think of, on top of protecting Teresa and trying to hold on to his sanity.

He dials the number and holds the receiver up to his ear for a minute. Nothing.

'Fucking useless!' he says. 'So much for their special service.'

'Call the guards go shopping Dunnes Stores!' his son reminds him.

'No, Brian,' Teresa says, still calm, knowing how enraged her answer is likely to make him.

He chews on his fist, always a bad sign. Just then, the lounge door opens and out bolts one of the neighbours' kids – I guess he'd been hiding in the computer room – and now he slips out the front door, closing it gently behind him.

'Go shopping Dunnes Stores!'

'Brian . . . ' I start but he turns and kicks in one of the panes of glass beside the front door.

'Go shopping Dunnes Stores!'

Another half-hour of this continues until all four of us are sitting in the kitchen. Brian's clothes couldn't be wetter if he'd been swimming in Galway Bay.

'Very sorry be good go shopping Dunnes Stores.'
'No.'
'Very sorry be good go shopping Dunnes Stores.'
'No,' his mother repeats.
'Very sorry be good go shopping Dunnes Stores.'

Such are the moments that pull and tear, that rip and pull a soul apart.

I THINK THAT the more time you spend in the company of an autistic person, the sooner you realise one great truth. Like many truths, it's not a particularly beautiful one at the time but it is the truth all the same.

And this is it: you hardly count. You register in their lives but not quite in the meaningful way you would like. In truth, you are just as normal, as demanding, strange, noisy and peculiar – and frightening – as any other.

He said it, not me.

I MUST ADMIT that there are times when the thought of being autistic has its appeal. There – I've said it.

The real world, that is the world we know through our senses to exist, is a scary place. The horrors of the world come at us on a tidal wave of blood and hysteria, terror and insane grief. There is too much noise, too much aggression; there is too much.

And, like the American Constitution, I hold these truths to be self-evident. If I was to be autistic, would that mean that I wouldn't be as sensitive to all this? The world is what you make it, of course. What I am getting at is this: if I were autistic would that enable me to avoid the hurt of, say, heartbreak?

For just as there is the physical act of killing, there is the other kind too: when the spirit is crushed. Myself I'd heard enough snide comments and enough cold laughter to last a lifetime. But if you took the cruelty in the world too personally, took it to your very core, it ended up killing you. I believed that. So I did my best to avoid such people. There is no greater loathing than that which others feel for themselves and feel impelled to communicate to you, whether you like it nor not.

But you can't get autism, the way you can 'get'

depression or schizophrenia. Besides, the so-called experts say that all the signs for autism are more or less apparent at age three or four. If you don't have the condition at that vulnerable age, then you're never going to get it, whatever you may wish.

All the same I think that the autistic embryo, foetus – call it what you like – the autistic *being* sensed deep truths about the world awaiting it from its first weeks in the mother's womb. It didn't like what it sensed of the world so decided to close itself off from it, making a mute protest, as a kind of battening-down of the hatches in the spirit, as it registered a deep disgust with the world and its motives.

And by doing this it made one thing impossible: a recognition of the love that awaited it 'out there'.

'Forget it!' the autistic seems to be saying. 'I'm not going out there like the rest. No. I'm going to seal myself off from all that, from their ways, their violence, their primitive rules of living. The world is a monster waiting to eat me. Better to stay the way I am. Much saner, safer, purer, that way.'

Probing the invisible,
touching truth.

I HAVE ALWAYS loved the summertime in Salthill. I love the smell of suntan oil as it wafts up from the beaches carried on a warm breeze, commingling with the smell of hot dogs and human pleasure. I like the way the black roads look in a heatwave, all sticky and popping and cracked. Even the tourists, loud Northerners with tattoos and belching from beer – loud and hungry in the Free State – even they have a certain rightness. They are on their holidays.

I am not on holiday. I am working; I am always working. For the last two months, I have taken on caring for two other boys, neither one autistic, but as charming and demanding in their own ways.

There are moments like now, as Brian and I leave the bus and pass by the Maxol station at Nile Lodge, when I want only to be away from the familiar world. I don't mean some anaesthetised autistic fantasy but away, away from all that is familiar. I want, need to be some place wholly unfamiliar. I want to be a tourist.

There is one question I am asked again and again: 'How do you do it?' They mean the job. And then they always add, 'Because I'd go crazy if I had to do what you do for a living.' Though they kindly do not remind me that I was never the most logical, linear or even rational of individuals, my mind always being aligned with the non-aligned.

'Me, I just wouldn't have the patience for your job.' That's something else I hear a lot.

They didn't know me before, when I was such an anxious, impatient, spoilt individual. The Brians of this world have in their own odd way been good for me.

It is no bad thing to slow down, to know how to take time, to wait.

Only now I think that I might be starting to crack up. No doubt quite a few of my problems have to do with this job. And it isn't just trying to break Brian out of his rituals and routines or the whole autistic conundrum.

No. I think it has something to do with an over-riding sense of failure, an admixture of guilt and shame, of not quite having the life I think I should have.

Also, an old Woody Allen quotation is in my mind: 'The last time I was inside a woman was when I visited the Statue of Liberty.' For all I know, I'm at my sexual prime. Then again, I've grown wary of women. I've had my heart broken once, but once is enough.

'I hate this job, Brian,' I say.

'Yeah,' he says, not looking at me.

'I need a break.'

'Break, yeah.'

'I mean ... Listen, what would you say, Brian, if I told you that tonight was the last time *ever* that I would take you out? What would you do then? No more Kev.'

'Kev, yeah.'

'No! No "*Kev yeah*," no Kev at all. In fact, Kev gone, gone *for ever*.'

We cross into Whitestrand Avenue. I have always been a fast walker; now I'm a fast walker-talker, yet realizing that this must be exactly what it's like to be a parent or a brother to an autistic child or young – or not so young – adult. You can't walk away from it.

'Who am I, Brian? Philosophically speaking, I mean? I don't have any money. No girlfriend. I admit that probably sounds shallow but I'm a *man*. I'm talking basic human needs here.'

'Yeah.'

And then I think about a travel book I've always meant to write. The trouble is, I actually detest travelling.

'Brian, I don't know what it is but it just seems like, these days, everything pisses me off. Frustrations, man. The thing is, I've got to get away. I mean it. Maybe I should go to India? No, the food would give me diarrhoea. I'd be better off disappearing up my own arse.'

'Yeah,' he says, eyes ahead.

'I have to do something radical, Brian. Fuck this job!'

And then something truly incredible, even fantastic, happens. He stops right there on the pavement, halts in full flight and looks quickly at me. Is that really concern I can read in his face? It was those last three words of mine that did it.

'Kev feel better?'

I reach out, pat him on the shoulder.

'Yeah, Brian. Kev feels better. God, it isn't your fault, mate. Honestly it isn't. You're a wonderful guy, Brian, and don't you ever forget it.'

'Feel better tomorrow?' Those blue-green eyes are wide with concern.

'Feel better tomorrow, yeah.'
And with that, we cross Grattan Road.

The seasons:
winter
spring
summer
autumn.
Regular.
Steady.
Ordered.
Autistic.

Something's wrong.

I follow him out of the house. All the signs are there for a mindstorm, and a bad one.

How do I know? By the way he runs ahead of me out of the estate, one half of his right fist jammed into his mouth. His teeth grind down on it, hard. 'Ahhhhhh! Brrrrr! Eeeeehhh!'

I catch up with him as he runs across the road. There's no way I'm going to take him on the bus like this, only to stand for ten or even twenty minutes at Nile Lodge while he paces and roars.

Maybe he'll cool off if we walk into town? Even as I think of doing just that, I know what a con that is. The man – he's nearly twenty – is set on full storm-mode. Nothing is going to alter its terrible course.

'Look, Brian, let's walk into town. You can get your stuff in Londis.' I'm thinking of the supermarket on the Father Griffin Road.

'No!' Never have I heard that tiny word screamed – yes, screamed – with greater anger or passion. Ian Paisley has nothing on him.

'Come on, let's go,' and I walk in the direction of town.

'Bus pass!'

I ignore him, walk on.

Suddenly, he has a can of Coke in his hands – where the hell did that come from? – and he screams, 'Throw it on the ground!'

And that's just what he does. He throws it full force to the pavement at the corner of Whitestrand Avenue. On the other pavement two couples passing by stare at him and move on.

I know I shouldn't do this but I do it all the same. I pick up the can. A tiny hole emits a thin spray of brown gunk into the air.

'Cut the shit!' I say, taking him by the arm and forcing him in the direction of town.

'Bus pass!'

'No! Now shut up and move!'

He actually runs off ahead of me, in the right direction, screaming like it's an Olympic event.

Because of the time of day, the roads and pavements are busy with people returning home from work. I really don't blame them for staring. I'd do the same myself, if I were one of them.

We actually make it as far as the traffic lights beside Maher's shop. In one direction, via the Crescent, is the bus-stop. But that's going backwards. We're all set to keep moving forward, that is, towards the Father Griffin Road which is only on the other side of the lights.

Brian's face is flushed. Tears are running down his face.

'Bus pass!'

He does what looks like a war-dance, all the while chewing on his fist and moaning.

I don't have any choice. I'll just have to lead him back

down the Crescent to the bus-stop. Who knows? We might actually make the bus.

He runs off in that direction anyway. I run to catch up with him, effing and blinding under my breath. I can imagine what we must both look like.

We manage to get as far as the traffic lights in time to see the bus drive by on green.

'Bus pass,' he wails. The driver can't not have heard him – most of them know us on this route – but he doesn't stop.

Well, that's it. We've no choice now but to walk. And he's seen the bus with his own eyes, so that in his not entirely illogical autistic way he has to accept it.

'Come on, Brian. We're going to walk into town. And don't give me any shit.'

He whips his Chicago Bears cap off his head and swipes at me with it. I duck just in time. He's bending to pick it up as I again cross the road into the Crescent. I note the grim irony of this address, known for its copper nameplates advertising psychiatrists, doctors, ortho-dontists. Maybe one of the shrinks is open?

He follows behind me – Brian, I mean, not a psy-chiatrist – as I turn left into Sea Road.

I'm glad it's dark. Somehow this sort of behaviour is worse in broad daylight.

'I'm going to call the guards if you keep this up! I fucking mean it, Brian.'

'Call the guards!' he cries as he lunges at me with his hat again. Then he sticks it into his mouth, chews on the bill, moans and writhes in his torment some more, suddenly switching to removing the cap and replacing it with his fist. Now he hammers with one hand at the other, and for an awful bitter moment, I'm reminded of Robert Crumb's brilliant, savage illustration to Charles Bukowski's brilliant, savage short story, 'Bring Me Your Love', the guy beating himself up by smashing his fist into his face.

Brian gains on me, forcing himself into my path. Then he lets rip with a scream. It's really something terrible this time, something so tortured and unnatural that even I'm startled by it. Even the youngsters standing outside the Jesuit School – unofficially the 'coolest' school in Galway – even they turn to look.

'Shut the fuck up!' I say.

'Shut up call the guards!'

Now he draws alongside me, everyone within ear- and eyeshot listening and watching. He is chewing on one of his thumbs and it suddenly occurs to me that this could be as much my reaction to Brian as his reaction to me. We have become mirror images of each other.

We pass into Lower Dominick Street, always a dreary hole, its godforsaken buildings that seem to lean in upon you, like something out of Hieronymus Bosch.

We cross the bridge and again I hear, 'Call the guards!'

I'm going to have to call someone. The Samaritans? They are in nearby Nuns' Island, after all. But the guards are closer, in Mill Street.

Finally, I decide to duck into the Left Bank café. He follows. I turn. 'Get your drink, sit down and shut up.'

'Coke?'

'Yeah.'

I go to the phone and his father answers. I tell Anthony

what's going down and that we'll probably be home sooner than usual. 'Fine,' he says, ever the stoic, and I imagine the strain on his kind face as he replaces the phone.

Brian sits muttering to himself at a table, watched closely by some of the assembled bohemians, who like to think they've seen it all. They've never been even touched.

I take a seat.

'Fruit Gums, Moro?' he asks, his breathing now less hurried.

'Go to the shop next door.'

'May I have a coffee?' I ask the woman behind the counter.

We have been making these evening outings for three years now. And, as usual, we stand at the Nile Lodge bus-stop.

'Isss eee bi ya!'

He's started again.

I watch him as he smiles and shakes his head from side to side. Now he claps his hands, peers into the gathering gloom. I even follow his gaze. What am I doing? Do I really expect to see something?

I listen, though. There are apparently four parts to the sentence: 'Isss eee bi ya!'

Is he by yer? No?

Issy biya? Issy biya. Not a lot of sense in that.

Izzie bya?

I go over it in my head of course (I'm the normal one around here, understand) and I think I can hear a name in there, somewhere.

Issy Beyer . . . German, perhaps?

Or Spanish? Izzy Baia. Now I know for a fact that, like Beyer, Baia is a legitimate surname, Spanish indeed. In the recent European Championships the Portuguese goalkeeper's name was Baia.

'Brian, who is Izzy Baia?'

He glances quickly at me, as though recognising the name.

'Izzy Baia!' he says, smiling.

What is he seeing that I can't see? What is he feeling, acknowledging, recognising that I can't feel, acknowledge or recognise? What is outside of my sensory range but within his?

We pass as shadows through
the space that is Autistland,
lightly, imperceptibly.
Unless you know how to look.

THE FIRST HOME I can remember was Staff Bungalow number 3, in the grounds of Bradwell Grove Mental Hospital in Oxfordshire. My parents were psychiatric nurses. Bradwell Grove was the name of that part of the Cotswolds we moved to from London.

During World War II, the hospital had been used as a supply depot by the US Army. Signs of the Allied occupation lay scattered in the long grass near the men's wards, odd bits and pieces like spent bullet-casings, faded webbed belts, strips of khaki and helmets curiously riddled with bullet holes. All these odd items were thrilling to inspect, examine, smell.

Nearby squatted redbrick bunkers, choked with weeds and thick clumps of grass but fun to scramble into and out of. Next to the bunkers were the oily rank depths of tank- and jeep-surviving ramps.

The Americans abandoned these ramshackle billets which stood windblown and sleepless, empty except for a few dented lockers, old metal bedframes and the broken halves of black Bakelite telephones. Inside them were heavy magnets. We'd never seen magnets before and wondered about them. How did they snap together like that? And why was it some resisted sticking together, however hard you pushed? These magnets would repel each other as if some invisible force-field wobbled in the air, stopping a connection from being made.

One mile from the bunkers and the billets was a long abandoned airstrip. It too was choked with weeds and grass and also dull dandelions, which sprouted up through cracks in the tar runway. Looming over the lot was the control tower, tall and empty and peeling white and beautiful in the sun.

As with the army stuff we stumbled upon, the airstrip made me think of American movies and Steve McQueen in *The Great Escape* and cool blokes in leather flying-jackets smoking fags and firing machine guns with one hand and laughing; the airstrip reeked of dead glamour and the musty smell of leather left too long in the scorching sun.

Occasionally, patients from the hospital would be drawn to us and want to go exploring. We weren't exactly sure what was wrong with them but we'd heard – though not from our parents – that there were words to describe them. Barmy was one; nutters, loonies, and headcases were others. We did not know that they were mentally handicapped. Nor did we know of the wards inside the hospital and their rows of beds and cots occupied by handicapped women and children.

Our mothers and fathers liked to see us playing with the patients. They had names that seemed to belong to another era: Bert, Ted, Arthur, George (nobody is called Bert, Ted, Arthur or George any more). They all had identical haircuts, razor-shorn very close to the nape of the neck, flecked with grey and combed through with a margarine slickness. It made them look much older than they actually were. When they were released from the wards we watched as they wandered around near the staff bungalows, a shifting mass in baggy suits that reeked of disinfectant, their tender faces either deeply tanned or badly sunburned, gazing into space, muttering and smiling at us, until, as two kinds of innocents, we were drawn back to each other.

There's a little of Izzy Baia
in each of you.
The thing to do is to know how
to look, in a new way, in a way
separate from the ways that went before.

It's a summer's evening. I'm walking up Quay Street when I see someone bearing a striking resemblance to Brian, only he's shed all the weight he put on over the year. So it can't be Brian, because he wouldn't be in town by himself. They say that everyone has a lookalike and here on this Saturday night I've found him.

We make eye contact and he smiles at me, motions me over to where he's standing outside Neachtain's bar.

'For a second there, I actually thought you were going to ignore me, Kev,' he says.

Now that I'm closer, I realise with a shock that it isn't someone who looks like Brian; it is Brian.

'Brian?'

'Yeah. Who did you think it was?' Gone from his voice is the dull autistic monotone. He has his father's good-humoured expression, a very Kerry thing, perhaps, that knows how ridiculous life is but what the hell? I really don't know what to say. I reach out, touch him. He's real; I'm not imagining this.

'It really is you, Brian. I thought I was looking at your double or something. And... Wait a second! Why aren't you at home? What are you doing here, tonight? Why... What... I think I need a drink.'

'Good idea. I'll tell you everything over a pint.'

We walk up Cross Street to Myles Lee's. Inside, we take seats in the back of the pub. It's quiet there.

Brian orders two Guinness. 'I'll bring them over,' says the barman.

'So...' Brian starts, a half-smile on his lips.

'This is really weird, Brian.'

'Well, Kev, I think I can understand how you feel. But I've been meaning to tell you, you and my family, that is.'

'Tell us what?' Our pints arrive but before Brian says anything, he takes a deep gulp from his glass. I do the same from mine.

He lets out a relieved gasp. Then he says, 'Kev, I never was autistic.'

Which makes sense – for now. Those perfectly phrased sentences, the sound of his voice, the fact that he's here, tonight, able to order – and pay for – two pints. The eye-contact.

'You were never autistic?' I say, slowly. None of this is right.

'Never.'

'So, let me get this straight: for the last twenty years you've been pretending to be autistic?' I lift my glass, take another swallow.

'You see, Kev, I really don't like to think of it as "pretending" per se, more like "coping". Yeah, coping is a better word.'

'You've been conning us. Me, your parents, your brothers, Eimear your sister, special-school teachers, experts, neighbours... Damn it, Brian, there's probably a law against that kind of thing.'

'I guess it was a con, an act, but it wasn't malicious. I really didn't mean any harm in it.' He finishes his pint as I finish mine. I stand, motion to the barman for more of the same, sit down again.

'But why, Brian? Why on earth would you do such a thing to the people who love you? It's crazy, is what it is.'

'Crazy?' And for a second, I catch a glimpse of the old Brian, Mr Mindstorm. Instead, he smiles patiently. 'Kev, I thought that you, of all people, would understand. You know as well as I do that "crazy" is right outside this bar, living among that lot,' and here he jerks a thumb in the direction of Cross Street. 'Out there is crazy, full of insane demands, greed, cruelty for the sake of cruelty.'

'Oh, hell, Brian, they're really not that bad.' But even as I say it I know how lame I must sound.

'Shite,' he says.' Look at you. You've always been a loner. Why do you think you got the job of being a carer anyway? Because someone could see that you're not like your average Joe, that there's something of that autistic detachment in yourself... But getting back to what I meant earlier. I thought that becoming autistic was a logical choice, a sane and sensible thing to do.'

'Like Birdy?'

'Who?'

'In the film by Alan Parker,' I say. 'It's based on the novel by William Wharton. It's about this guy Birdy who becomes traumatised in the war – in the book it's World War II, in the movie, Vietnam – and when he returns to America he spends most of his time squatting in a military psychiatric hospital pretending to be a canary, while his buddy Al, played brilliantly by Nicholas Cage, tries to talk

*him out of it and back into the real world he's left behind.
Matthew Modine was Birdy and he was terrific.'*

*'Yeah, well. Birdy ... I guess you could draw parallels
with me and all the others.'*

'What "others"?'

*'The so-called autistic. Who else?' He smiles as the
barman returns with fresh pints. I pay him.*

*'Wait a second here,' I say, draining off half the pint.
'You're saying that all the other autistics, in Ireland and
everywhere else, are pretending too?'*

*'Sounds sane to me. We're inhabitants of Autistland,
where everything is just as it should be and no one is
afraid to be themselves.'*

'But that's completely insane! I need another drink.'

*'"Insane?" Listen to yourself, Kev! Just take a look at
the world at large!'*

*'All right, the world isn't perfect. But just because it
stops being beautiful for you doesn't stop it being beautiful
for others. There's never been a creature as fascinating,
as complex, as brilliant as man. As I may have said before,
like the American Constitution, Brian, I hold these truths
to be self-evident.'*

*'So what have I missed? What do you see that I can't
see?'*

*I drain my Guinness, motion for two more. Brian
finishes his, looks at me, his face serious, alert. He's
listening.*

*'Brian, don't think that I haven't been hurt by life or
disgusted by human nature; I have. And on more occasions
that you'd know. But I've seen the other side, too. I'm
talking about human selflessness: aid-workers, young*

people who sacrifice careers and material gain, and other things, to devote their lives to the starving, the oppressed. Doctors, nurses, relief crews, engineers ... You name it. People! Beautiful, fantastic people! Heroes, Brian! They work for the Red Cross, for Amnesty International. They give up their time and money for the homeless, for peace and justice for the poor. They don't do it for the attention, for money, but for deeper reasons that maybe can't be fully articulated.

'Take my own life. I've lost count of the times I've been disgusted by people's lies, their treachery, their snideness, hypocrisy, their shitty little smiles that seem to hint at something you can only guess at, the cowardliness of the mob mentality. So often, I've wanted only to say, "Fuck it! I want nothing more to do with the human race," until ... something happens. It might be nothing more than seeing a pretty girl crossing a busy road and the way she moves, the way she glances but briefly at you, when a stranger, for example, someone you've never met does an act of kindness, of selflessness, just for you, wanting or asking for nothing in return. My life, Brian, has been changed more than you or even I will ever know by the heroism of so-called ordinary people. They redeem their world by their actions. And it isn't just strangers. My life has been made fuller, happier, by books, by movies, by silly songs, by true stories of goodness and altruism.

It's as if God, life – call it what you want – is speaking through these moments, saying, "Hang in there; we need you." You see, Brian, people are just people. As far as I'm concerned there are actually only four kinds and this goes for every religion, race and ethnic group: good people, bad people, good people who occasionally act like the bad, who are bastards, and bad people who suddenly behave in a way that is revelatory, wonderful, angelic even. Four types. That's all the world is made up of. The world is just there, Brian, neither always good nor always bad. Now, you know I do a lot of cycling. And often I'm pedalling along the prom in a force-eight gale and I've cursed that cold wind. But wait: on my return journey that wind is on my back, is my friend, pushing me towards home.

'Meetings and moments, Brian. Like sitting opposite a beautiful young woman. And this has happened to me and will happen to you, too. She's right there in front of you. She is wearing a perfume called Joop. And she is telling you about a particularly funny, if hair-raising, moment in her life, when she was a visitor, alone, in New York City and as she talks she takes your hands in hers and, very unselfconsciously, she holds and strokes them, and you know, man, you just know that in that moment your life has been changed for ever and all the hurt of the past disappears, dwindles, becomes nothing. Because it's love, you see. And you know it just then, in that touch she has, and maybe she knows it too but you don't say anything, only go on listening, savouring the moment, knowing that your life is changed now and for ever, amen, as if a secret had been passed on to you: this is how a life should always be: sacred, as perfect and decent as this moment.

'I think, Brian, that every life must be composed of these moments born of love. But you can only know that by being out there! Being part of life, no matter how shitty and random and cruel it can get, because waiting always is beauty, is an ending to what hurts and injures.'

I stop, drink some more, my head woozy. I'm not sure I've made much sense.

He finishes his third pint. 'I need to go to the toilet. But I'll be thinking about what you said.'

'Great. I'll go and get in some more drinks.'

I stand and go to the bar. The guy behind the counter is watching me curiously. I don't give a damn. I'm wondering, though, how Brian is going to break the news to Anthony and Teresa that he isn't what they always thought he was.

I return to our table with two more pints. Brian's sitting there, looking around him.

'Maybe we should take it easy on the booze,' I say, but he doesn't respond, only watches me blankly. He is gone again and this time there's no pretending. I put my head down on the table. I could cry. I could have found out the truth about Izzy Baia while I was going on and on and didn't. And now it's too late.

Dream segue,
breaking the illusion.

It's RAINING and Anthony insists on driving us into town.

Brian sits behind me, no longer the sixteen-year-old from all those years ago in Eason's leafing through the Red Cross book. He recently celebrated his twenty-first birthday.

His weekdays are spent in a special training centre. He is learning how to make rugs, bird tables and bookshelves.

And he hasn't had a mindstorm in months.

But mindstorms or no mindstorms, he's still autistic. I suppose that you expected him to change in some radical way, to emerge from his autism like Birdy emerged from his trauma.

Dream on.

If you want a happy ending, read a fairytale.

'Now' is all that exists. And now, as we pull out of the drive, is contentment. And that's not so bad.

'How's Briny?' his father asks, looking back at him. I look at Anthony, thinking, so this is what a hero looks like? And a heroine stands inside the kitchen making dinner. And what of his brothers, Niall and Enda, who have had to put up with so much from their eldest brother, not least in the form of physical and verbal hammerings? Heroes both. Stoics. Living wonders. And sister Eimear, who fought for Brian more than once as they were growing up, who defended him, looked after him and never once said a word to me or anyone but her family about it. It was a privilege to know them. I had been blessed. That's all there was to it. And, I think, somewhere during all those afternoons and evenings, I had redeemed something in myself. I had made a modest improvement in the quality of Brian's life just as he had made a major difference to mine. If you think that what you do ultimately matters, then in time it will, in ways you might never have anticipated.

The car moves on to the main road as Brian asks, 'Dubliners' tape?'

His father reaches for the cassette, slips it into the tape deck. Music surrounds us.

AFTERWORD

I hope that *Izzy Baia* has broadened your understanding of autism and perhaps made you consider this curious condition in another way. Brian O'Connor may be autistic, but he's still an individual. He is not an autistic Everyman.

For information on autism in Ireland, Britain and Europe, please contact:

The Irish Society for Autism
Unity Building
16–17 Lr O'Connell Street
Dublin 1

The National Autistic Society
276 Willesden Lane
London NW2 5RB